HOW TO BUILD A MACHINE LEARNING MODEL

From Concept to Creation: Crafting Your Machine Learning Model.

LYNNE RUFFIN

Table of contents

Introduction to Machine Learning

Mimicked knowledge, a subset of man-made thinking, is upsetting different associations by empowering PCs to procure from information and seek after suppositions or choices without being unequivocally different. It integrates a substitute arrangement of systems and assessments that permit PCs to see models and concentrate snippets of data from huge datasets. Understanding the fundamentals of man-made consciousness is essential for the two young people and experienced experts needing to saddle its power in dealing with complex issues across locales.

Understanding the Basics

At its center, man-made knowledge depends upon assessments that iteratively gain from information to cultivate execution on a particular undertaking moreover. These calculations can be broadly gathered into three sorts: oversaw learning, solo learning, and sponsorship learning.

Coordinated learning consolidates setting up a model on a stepped dataset, where every information point is associated with a checking out at objective or result. The model sorts out a smart method for planning input parts to the right result considering the gave marks. Normal controlled learning assignments solidify assembling and break faith.

Free learning, obviously, regulates unlabeled information and plans to find stowed away models or plans inside the dataset.

Clustering and dimensionality decline are normal execution learning assignments, where the objective is to pack essentially indistinguishable data of interest or diminish the complex idea of the information.

Support learning consolidates setting up a specialist to assist a climate to heighten joined rewards. The master learns through experimentation, getting investigation as remunerations or disciplines thinking about its activities. Support learning has applications in areas like gaming, significant level mechanics, and independent vehicles.

Importance and Applications

The making importance of PC based knowledge starts from its capacity to eliminate huge snippets of data from information and robotize dynamic cycles. In the ongoing information driven world, relationship across different associations are utilizing recreated knowledge to get a benefit and drive headway.

In clinical advantages, man-made knowledge is being utilized to moreover encourage diagnostics, re-try treatment designs, and anticipate patient results. By isolating electronic success records and clinical imaging information, recreated knowledge models can help clinical thought suppliers in early ailment region and treatment improvement.

In finance, man-made reasoning assessments are utilized for bending recognizing confirmation, risk assessment, and algorithmic exchanging. These models research tremendous extents of cash related information to see false exchanges, evaluate credit risk, and advance undertaking methodologies.

In showing and propelling, PC based knowledge is used for client division, changed thoughts, and alloted publicizing. By dismantling client lead and propensities, PC based insight calculations connect with relationship to give more critical and drawing in satisfied to their optimal vested party.

In gathering, reproduced knowledge anticipates a pivotal part in discerning assistance, quality control, and store network improvement. By dissecting sensor information from hardware and creation processes, man-made knowledge models can anticipate gear disappointments and upset expensive individual time.

In frame, man-made consciousness has changed into a basic mechanical gathering for dealing with complex issues and driving progression across different associations. By understanding the fundamentals of PC based knowledge and its applications, people and affiliations can open its most outrageous capacity to choose worth and go with informed choices in an information driven world.

Chapter One

Getting Started

Building a man-made intelligence model requires careful planning, data on various instruments and designs, and an especially planned improvement environment. In this helper, we will research the central stages in any case constructing a computer based intelligence model, including setting up your momentum situation and picking the right gadgets and situation.

Setting Up Your Environment

Before diving into building a man-made intelligence model, it's basic to set up your improvement environment to ensure smooth execution and reliable blend of gadgets and libraries. Here are the basic stages to setting up your ongoing situation:

1. ***Pick a Programming Language:*** Python is the most renowned programming language for simulated intelligence as a result of its straightforwardness, wide libraries, and dynamic neighborhood. Present Python and a pack chief like Boa constrictor to supervise libraries and conditions successfully.

2. ***Present Required Libraries:*** Key libraries for artificial intelligence in Python consolidate NumPy for numerical handling, pandas for data control, matplotlib and seaborn for data discernment, and scikit-learn for artificial intelligence estimations. Use pip or conda to present these libraries.

3. ***Set Up Integrated Headway Environment (IDE):*** Pick an IDE that

suits your tendencies and work process. Notable decisions consolidate Jupyter Diary for instinctive new development, PyCharm for a total Python IDE, and VSCode for lightweight coding with extensions for Python improvement.

4. ***Organize Variation Control:*** Transformation control is crucial for administering code changes and collaborating with others. Set up a structure control system like Git and pick a working with stage like GitHub or GitLab to store your code vaults and track changes.

Picking the Right Mechanical assemblies and Designs:

Picking the right gadgets and designs is dire for building a man-made intelligence model that meets your requirements and performs preferably. Think about the going with components while picking gadgets and frameworks:

1. ***Task and Space:*** Recognize the specific task you want to handle with artificial intelligence and the region you are working in. Different endeavors and spaces could require different contraptions and designs overhauled for unequivocal use cases.

2. ***Flexibility and Execution:*** Survey the versatility and execution necessities of your man-made intelligence model. Pick instruments and frameworks that can manage gigantic datasets and

complex models actually, especially expecting you are working with immense data or prevalent execution enlisting conditions.

3. **Neighborhood Sponsorship:** Ponder the size and activity of the neighborhood a particular instrument or design. An exuberant neighborhood give significant resources, documentation, and support for researching issues and learning new methodologies.

4. **Fuse with Existing Structures:** Expecting you are planning computer based intelligence into existing structures or work processes, pick devices and frameworks that perfectly coordinate with your ongoing establishment and advances.

5. **Flexibility and Customization:** Study the versatility and customization

decisions introduced by different devices and designs. Pick ones that grant you to re-try and change your models according to your specific essentials and necessities.

Choosing the Right Tools and Frameworks

A couple of notable gadgets and frameworks are extensively used in the artificial intelligence social class for building and sending artificial intelligence models. Here are without a doubt the most consistently used ones:

1. ***TensorFlow:*** Made by Google, TensorFlow is an open-source artificial intelligence framework that gives a broad climate of gadgets and libraries for building and sending man-made intelligence models. It is

extensively used for significant learning endeavors and offers unrivaled execution and versatility.

2. **PyTorch:** Made by Facebook, PyTorch is an open-source man-made intelligence framework known for its dynamic computational diagram and intuitive Programming connection point. It is notable among experts and experts for its flexibility and ease of use, especially for prototyping and experimentation.

3. **Scikit-learn:** scikit-learn is an essential and useful simulated intelligence library in view of top of NumPy, SciPy, and matplotlib. It gives countless estimations and instruments for oversaw and independent learning, model evaluation, and data preprocessing.

4. ***Keras:*** Keras is an evident level cerebrum networks Programming connection point written in Python and fit for running on top of TensorFlow, Theano, or Microsoft Mental Apparatus compartment (CNTK). It is expected for speedy experimentation and prototyping of significant learning models with a straightforward connection point.

Setting up your ongoing situation and picking the right gadgets and designs are essential pushes toward building a computer based intelligence model successfully. By noticing the principles outlined in this associate and considering your specific essentials and objectives, you can lay out the preparation for a compelling computer based intelligence undertaking and open the ability of this completely exhilarating field.

Chapter Two

Data Preparation

Information planning is a pivotal move toward building an AI model that can create exact forecasts and experiences. It includes gathering, investigating, cleaning, and preprocessing information to guarantee its quality, significance, and reasonableness for the planned errand. In this aide, we will investigate the fundamental parts of information planning, including information assortment and investigation, as well as information cleaning and preprocessing procedures.

Data Collection and Exploration

Information assortment is the method involved with get-together pertinent datasets from different sources, including data sets, APIs, records, and outside vaults. It is fundamental for gather extensive and delegate information that enough covers the objective space and incorporates significant elements for the AI task.

When the information is gathered, the subsequent stage is information investigation, which includes examining and figuring out the construction, dispersion, and qualities of the dataset. Information investigation recognizes possible examples, abnormalities, and bits of knowledge that can illuminate ensuing strides in the information readiness process.

Key parts of information investigation include

1. ***Unmistakable Measurements:*** Register illustrative insights like mean, middle, standard deviation, and quartiles for mathematical highlights to grasp their focal propensity and scattering.

2. ***Information Perception:*** Imagine the dispersion of mathematical elements utilizing histograms, box plots, and dissipate plots. Imagine connections between highlights utilizing relationship lattices and match plots.

3. ***Include Designing:*** Make new highlights or change existing elements to improve the prescient force of the model. Highlight designing methods incorporate one-hot encoding for all out factors, scaling for mathematical

factors, and making cooperation or polynomial elements.

Data Cleaning and Preprocessing

Information cleaning is the most common way of identifying and remedying mistakes, irregularities, and missing qualities in the dataset to guarantee its honesty and dependability. Information preprocessing includes changing the crude information into a configuration reasonable for AI calculations by applying different procedures like standardization, normalization, and component scaling.

Key parts of information cleaning and preprocessing include:

1. *Taking care of Missing Qualities:* Distinguish and deal with missing

qualities in the dataset by crediting them with mean, middle, or mode values, or utilizing progressed procedures, for example, k-closest neighbors (KNN) ascription or prescient displaying.

2. ***Anomaly Location and Treatment:*** Recognize exceptions in the dataset utilizing factual strategies, for example, z-score, IQR (interquartile reach), or perception procedures, for example, box plots. Treat anomalies by eliminating them, changing them, or utilizing vigorous measurable techniques.

3. ***Encoding Straight out Factors:*** Convert unmitigated factors into mathematical arrangement utilizing strategies, for example, one-hot encoding, mark encoding, or ordinal encoding,

contingent upon the idea of the clear cut factors and the necessities of the AI calculation.

4. ***Include Scaling***: Scale mathematical elements to a comparative reach utilizing procedures, for example, min-max scaling or normalization. Scaling guarantees that elements with bigger extents don't overwhelm the model's way of learning.

5. ***Dimensionality Decrease***: Lessen the dimensionality of the dataset by eliminating superfluous or repetitive elements utilizing procedures like head part examination (PCA) or highlight choice strategies in light of measurable tests or AI calculations.

Information readiness is a basic move toward building an AI model that can create exact forecasts and bits of knowledge. By following the fundamental advances framed in this aide, including information assortment and investigation, as well as information cleaning and preprocessing strategies, you can guarantee that your dataset is of top notch and appropriate for preparing AI models. Compelling information readiness establishes the groundwork for effective model preparation and assessment, prompting powerful and solid AI arrangements.

Chapter Three

Model Selection

Model choice is a basic move toward building an AI model that can really tackle a particular undertaking or issue. It includes grasping various calculations, their assets, shortcomings, and reasonableness for the job needing to be done, and choosing the most fitting model in light of different rules like exactness, interpretability, adaptability, and computational effectiveness. In this aide, we will investigate the course of model determination, including figuring out various calculations, assessing their exhibition, and picking the right model for your undertaking.

Understanding Different Algorithms

AI calculations can be comprehensively ordered into three principal types: directed learning, unaided learning, and support learning. Each sort of calculation is appropriate for various kinds of assignments and information, and understanding their qualities is vital for compelling model choice.

Directed Learning Calculations:

Regulated gaining calculations gain from named information, where every information point is related with a comparing objective or result. Normal regulated learning calculations include:

- ***Straight Relapse:*** A relapse calculation utilized for anticipating ceaseless mathematical qualities in light of info highlights.

- ***Calculated Relapse:*** A characterization calculation utilized for foreseeing paired or multi-class unmitigated qualities in view of information highlights.

- ***Choice Trees:*** A tree-based calculation that parcels the information space into districts and settles on forecasts in light of straightforward choice principles at every hub.

- ***Irregular Woodland:*** An outfit calculation that consolidates different choice trees to work on prescient execution and lessen overfitting.

Unaided Learning Calculations:

Solo gaining calculations gain from unlabeled information and mean to find stowed away examples or designs inside the dataset. Normal solo learning calculations include:

- **K-implies Bunching**: A grouping calculation that parcels the information into k groups in view of closeness measures.

- **Head Part Investigation (PCA)**: A dimensionality decrease procedure that projects high-layered information onto a lower-layered subspace while protecting the fluctuation.

- **Gaussian Blend Models (GMMs)**: A probabilistic model that addresses the information as a combination of a few Gaussian circulations.

Support Learning Calculations:

Support gaining calculations gain from connection with a climate to boost aggregate prizes. Normal support learning calculations include:

- **Q-Learning**: A without model support learning calculation that learns an ideal strategy by iteratively refreshing Q-values in view of noticed rewards.

- **_Profound Q-Organizations (DQN):_** A profound learning-based support learning calculation that consolidates Q-learning with profound brain organizations to deal with high-layered state spaces.

- **_Strategy Slope Techniques:_** Support learning calculations that straightforwardly enhance the arrangement capability to amplify anticipated rewards, for example, Build up and Proximal Approach Improvement (PPO).

Choosing the Right Model for Your Task

When you have a fundamental comprehension of various calculations, the following stage is to pick the right model for your particular undertaking in view of different standards, for example,

1. ***Nature of the Errand:*** Decide if the undertaking is a relapse issue (foreseeing consistent qualities), characterization issue (foreseeing all out values), or bunching issue (gathering comparative pieces of information).

2. ***Intricacy of the Model:*** Consider the intricacy of the model expected for the errand. For straightforward assignments with direct connections, direct relapse or strategic relapse might get the job done. For complex

errands with non-direct connections, more refined models like choice trees, arbitrary timberlands, or profound learning models might be required.

3. ***Interpretability***: Consider the interpretability of the model and whether partners should grasp how the model makes expectations. Direct relapse and choice trees are more interpretable contrasted with complex models like profound learning models.

4. ***Execution***: Assess the exhibition of various models utilizing suitable execution measurements and approval strategies like cross-approval. Pick the model that accomplishes the best exhibition on the approval dataset

5. ***Versatility***: Consider the adaptability of the model concerning the size of the dataset and computational assets

accessible. A few calculations might scale better to huge datasets or conveyed processing conditions than others.

6. ***Space Information:*** Consider area explicit information and bits of knowledge that might impact the decision of model. For instance, assuming the undertaking includes picture acknowledgment, convolutional brain organizations (CNNs) are ordinarily involved because of their viability in dealing with spatial information.

Model choice is a basic move toward building an AI model that can successfully take care of a particular errand or issue. By figuring out various calculations, their qualities, and reasonableness for the main job, and assessing their exhibition in view of different rules like precision, interpretability, adaptability, and computational proficiency, you can pick the right model that meets the prerequisites of your undertaking and conveys ideal execution. Powerful model choice establishes the groundwork for building fruitful AI models that drive development and tackle genuine issues across spaces.

Chapter Four

Model Training

Model preparation is an essential move toward building an AI model that can settle on exact expectations or choices in light of information. It includes choosing a suitable calculation, preparing the model on a marked dataset, and streamlining its boundaries to accomplish ideal execution. In this aide, we will investigate the fundamental parts of model preparation, including dividing information for preparing and testing, as well as tuning hyperparameters for ideal execution.

Splitting Data for Training and Testing

Parting the dataset into preparing and testing subsets is an essential move toward model preparation to assess its exhibition on inconspicuous information and forestall overfitting. The preparation dataset is utilized to prepare the model, while the testing dataset is utilized to assess its exhibition on concealed information. Normal strategies for dividing information include:

1. **Train-Test Split:** The dataset is haphazardly partitioned into preparing and testing subsets utilizing a predefined proportion, like 70-30 or 80-20. The preparation subset is utilized to prepare the model, while the testing subset is utilized to assess its presentation.

2. **Cross-Approval:** Cross-approval is a more vigorous strategy for dividing information, particularly for little datasets. It includes partitioning the dataset into k subsets (overlays) and performing k cycles, each time involving k-1 folds for preparing and the excess overlap for testing.

3. *Defined Examining:* Separated testing guarantees that the class conveyance in the preparation and testing subsets is illustrative of the generally dataset, particularly for imbalanced datasets with inconsistent class extents.

Dividing the information into preparing and testing subsets evaluates the model's speculation execution and distinguish potential issues, for example, overfitting or underfitting.

Tuning Hyperparameters for Optimal Performance

Hyperparameters are boundaries that are not mastered during the preparation interaction yet are set prior to preparing and influence the way of behaving and execution of the model. Tuning hyperparameters includes finding the ideal qualities or mixes of values that expand the model's presentation on the approval or testing dataset.

Normal methods for tuning hyperparameters include:

1. **_Lattice Search:_** Framework search includes characterizing a network of hyperparameter esteems and assessing the model's exhibition for every mix of values utilizing cross-approval. The mix of hyperparameters that yields the best

exhibition score is chosen as the ideal arrangement.

2. ***Irregular Hunt:*** Arbitrary inquiry haphazardly tests hyperparameter values from predefined circulations and assesses the model's presentation for each examined design utilizing cross-approval. Irregular inquiry is more effective than lattice look for high-layered hyperparameter spaces.

3. ***Bayesian Streamlining:*** Bayesian improvement is a probabilistic enhancement method that models the goal capability (model execution) as a probabilistic substitute and iteratively chooses hyperparameter values to limit the normal misfortune. Bayesian enhancement is effective for black-box streamlining issues with boisterous or costly goal capabilities.

4. ***Robotized Hyperparameter Tuning:*** Computerized hyperparameter tuning instruments and libraries, for example, scikit-enhance, Hyperopt, and Optuna, give mechanized and effective techniques to hyperparameter streamlining utilizing different calculations and search methodologies.

Model preparation is a basic move toward building an AI model that can settle on exact expectations or choices in light of information. By dividing the information into preparing and testing subsets and tuning hyperparameters for ideal execution, you can guarantee that your model sums up well to inconspicuous information and accomplishes the ideal degree of exactness and dependability. Viable model preparation establishes the groundwork for sending AI models in certifiable applications and taking care of mind boggling issues across areas.

Chapter Five

Model Evaluation

Model assessment is a basic move toward building an AI model that can settle on exact expectations or choices in view of info information. It includes surveying the model's presentation utilizing different execution measurements and assessment strategies, deciphering the outcomes, and iteratively working on the model to accomplish ideal execution. In this aide, we will investigate the fundamental parts of model assessment, including execution measurements and assessment methods, as well as deciphering results and iterative improvement techniques.

Performance Metrics and Evaluation Techniques

Execution measurements and assessment strategies are utilized to evaluate the quality and viability of an AI model in pursuing forecasts or choices. They give quantitative proportions of the model's presentation across various angles, for example, exactness, accuracy, review, F1 score, and region under the collector working trademark (ROC) bend. Normal execution measurements and assessment procedures include:

1. **Precision:** Exactness estimates the extent of accurately arranged cases out of the complete number of examples in the dataset. It is a basic and natural measurement yet may not be reasonable for imbalanced datasets

where the classes are not similarly addressed.

2. ***Accuracy and Review***: Accuracy estimates the extent of genuine positive cases among all examples named positive by the model, while review estimates the extent of genuine positive occasions accurately recognized by the model out of all real certain occurrences. Accuracy and review are frequently utilized together to assess the compromise between bogus up-sides and misleading negatives.

3. **F1 Score**: F1 score is the consonant mean of accuracy and review and gives a decent proportion of a model's presentation, particularly in imbalanced datasets. It considers both bogus up-sides and misleading

negatives and is especially helpful when the class dissemination is slanted.

4. ***ROC Bend and AUC-ROC:*** The recipient working trademark (ROC) bend plots the genuine positive rate (TPR) against the misleading positive rate (FPR) at different limit settings. The region under the ROC bend (AUC-ROC) measures the model's capacity to recognize positive and negative occasions, with a higher AUC-ROC showing better execution.

5. ***Disarray Lattice:*** A disarray network is an even portrayal of the model's expectations versus the real class marks in the dataset. It gives experiences into the model's presentation across various classes and works with the estimation of

different execution measurements like exactness, accuracy, review, and F1 score.

Interpreting Results and Iterative Improvement

Deciphering the after effects of model assessment is fundamental for figuring out the model's assets, shortcomings, and regions for development. It includes investigating the exhibition measurements, assessing the model's conduct on various subsets of information, and distinguishing possible wellsprings of mistakes or predispositions.

Key parts of deciphering results and iterative improvement include:

1. ***Dissecting Execution Measurements:*** Look at the upsides of execution measurements like exactness,

accuracy, review, and F1 score to evaluate the model's general presentation and distinguish regions for development. Think about the model's presentation against pattern models or benchmarks to check its viability.

2. ***Researching Mistakes and Predispositions***: Dissect the disarray network and analyze misclassified occurrences to distinguish examples, patterns, or predispositions in the model's expectations. Examine likely wellsprings of blunders like imbalanced information, loud highlights, or mislabeled occurrences, and make remedial moves to address them.

3. ***Cross-Approval and Model Choice***: Perform cross-approval to survey the

model's security and speculation execution across various subsets of information. Look at the presentation of different models utilizing cross-approval and select the best-performing model in light of predefined measures.

4. ***Hyperparameter Tuning***: Calibrate the model's hyperparameters utilizing strategies, for example, network search, arbitrary pursuit, or Bayesian streamlining to work on its exhibition on the approval or testing dataset. Try different things with various hyperparameter setups and assess their effect on the model's presentation.

5. ***Troupe Techniques***: Investigate gathering strategies like stowing, supporting, or stacking to join

different models and work on prescient execution. Gathering techniques influence the variety of individual models to decrease fluctuation and further develop speculation execution.

Iterative improvement is a continuous interaction that includes refining the model, integrating input from model assessment, and repeating on the plan and execution to accomplish ideal execution.

Model assessment is a basic move toward building an AI model that can pursue exact expectations or choices in view of information. By utilizing execution measurements and assessment strategies to survey the model's presentation, deciphering the outcomes, and iteratively working on the model, you can guarantee that your model accomplishes ideal execution and sums up well to concealed information. Powerful model assessment establishes the groundwork for conveying AI models in true applications and tackling complex issues across areas.

Chapter Six

Deployment and Beyond

Sending is the zenith of the AI model improvement process, denoting the change from trial and error to certifiable application. Nonetheless, fruitful sending is only the start of a model's lifecycle. Past organization, it is vital for screen the model's presentation, assemble criticism, and constantly further develop it to guarantee its viability and pertinence in genuine situations. In this aide, we will investigate the basic parts of conveying an AI model in certifiable situations, checking its exhibition, and accomplishing ceaseless improvement.

Deploying Your Model in Real-world Scenarios

Sending an AI model includes coordinating it into existing frameworks or work processes to robotize dynamic cycles or create forecasts continuously. It requires cautious thought of different variables, including adaptability, dependability, security, and ease of use. Here are the key advances engaged with sending an AI model in true situations:

1. ***Foundation Arrangement***: Pick a suitable framework for conveying the model, taking into account factors like computational assets, stockpiling prerequisites, and versatility. Choices incorporate cloud stages (e.g., AWS, Purplish blue, Google Cloud), on-premises servers, or edge gadgets.

2. ***Model Bundling***: Bundle the prepared model alongside any fundamental preprocessing or post-handling ventures into a deployable configuration, like a Docker holder or a serialized model document (e.g., pickle, ONNX).

3. ***Combination with Existing Frameworks***: Incorporate the conveyed model into existing frameworks or work processes, guaranteeing similarity with information sources, APIs, and UIs. This might include creating APIs for model induction, carrying out information pipelines for taking care of info information to the model, or incorporating with UIs for showing results.

4. ***Testing and Approval***: Completely test the sent model in an organizing climate to guarantee its usefulness, unwavering quality, and execution under different circumstances. Approve the model's results against ground truth or human specialists to confirm its precision and consistency.

5. ***Checking and Logging***: Carry out observing and logging systems to follow the model's presentation, utilization, and blunders progressively. Screen key measurements like derivation dormancy, throughput, asset usage, and forecast precision to recognize execution corruption or abnormalities.

6. ***Security and Consistence***: Execute safety efforts to safeguard delicate information and guarantee

consistence with pertinent guidelines (e.g., GDPR, HIPAA). Secure information transmission, scramble model boundaries, and carry out access controls to forestall unapproved access or altering.

Monitoring and Continuous Improvement

When conveyed, the AI model enters a period of persistent observing and improvement to keep up with its viability and pertinence in certifiable situations. Observing includes following the model's presentation, gathering input from clients, and recognizing valuable open doors for development. Ceaseless improvement includes repeating on the model plan, refreshing preparation information, and retraining the model to adjust to changing circumstances and necessities. Here are the vital parts of observing and ceaseless improvement:

1. **Execution Observing:** Constantly screen the model's presentation measurements and key pointers to recognize deviations from anticipated conduct. Set up robotized cautions and dashboards to advise partners of execution debasement or irregularities.

2. **Client Criticism and Iterative Improvement:** Assemble input from clients, space specialists, and partners to distinguish regions for development and focus on highlight demands or bug fixes. Integrate client criticism into model updates and emphasize on the model plan in like manner.

3. ***Information Quality and Float Location:*** Screen the nature of info information and identify information float or idea float that might influence the model's exhibition. Carry out information approval checks, information float identification calculations, and retraining triggers to keep up with information quality and model precision over the long haul.

4. ***Model Retraining and Forming:*** Routinely retrain the model utilizing refreshed or expanded preparing information to work on its exhibition and adjust to developing examples or patterns in the information. Execute model forming and rollback components to follow model changes and return to past renditions if vital.

5. **A/B Testing and Trial and error:** Direct A/B tests and investigations to assess the effect of model changes on key execution measurements and client fulfillment. Think about various model adaptations or setups and take on the ones that yield the best outcomes.

6. *Lifecycle The executives:* Deal with the whole lifecycle of the conveyed model, including adaptation control, documentation, and filing. Monitor model forms, try results, and sending history to work with coordinated effort, reproducibility, and auditability.

Sending and past are basic stages in the lifecycle of an AI model, denoting the progress from advancement to certifiable application and persistent improvement. By conveying the model in certifiable situations, checking its exhibition, and accomplishing constant improvement through iterative turn of events, associations can guarantee that their AI models stay successful, dependable, and applicable in resolving complex issues and conveying esteem in assorted spaces. Viable sending and constant improvement processes are fundamental for expanding the effect of AI models and driving advancement in true applications.

Chapter Seven

Case Studies and Examples

Real-life Examples and Applications

AI has become progressively predominant in different ventures, altering processes, and empowering creative answers for complex issues. Genuine models and contextual analyses give important experiences into how AI is applied practically speaking and feature its assorted applications across spaces. In this aide, we will investigate genuine models and contextual analyses of AI applications, exhibiting the way things are utilized to take care of certifiable issues and drive advancement.

Medical services:

AI is changing medical services by empowering customized therapy plans, early infection location, and prescient examination. One eminent model is the utilization of AI calculations to dissect clinical imaging information, like X-beams and X-rays, for early discovery of sicknesses like malignant growth. Organizations like Google Wellbeing and IBM Watson Wellbeing have created AI models that can precisely distinguish irregularities in clinical pictures, helping radiologists in diagnosing illnesses and working on understanding results.

Finance:

In the money business, AI is utilized for misrepresentation identification, risk appraisal, and algorithmic exchanging. Monetary establishments influence AI calculations to investigate exchange information and recognize dubious examples demonstrative of fake exercises. For instance, banks use AI models to identify

Mastercard extortion by breaking down exchange history, client conduct, and exchange metadata continuously. Via mechanizing misrepresentation recognition processes, AI assists monetary organizations with limiting misfortunes and safeguard clients' resources.

Online business:

AI assumes a vital part in further developing client experience and driving deals in the online business industry. Organizations like Amazon and Netflix use AI calculations to give customized proposals to clients in view of their perusing history, buy conduct, and inclinations. These proposal frameworks examine enormous volumes of information to recognize designs and anticipate client inclinations, assisting clients with finding pertinent items or content and expanding commitment and transformation rates.

Transportation:

In the transportation area, AI is utilized for course improvement, prescient upkeep, and independent vehicles. Organizations like Uber and Lyft use AI calculations to streamline ride-sharing courses, limit travel time, and coordinate drivers with travelers effectively. Independent vehicle organizations like Waymo and Tesla influence AI models for continuous discernment, direction, and control, empowering vehicles to explore complex conditions and work securely without human mediation.

Hands-on Projects for Practice

Involved projects give important chances to rehearsing AI abilities, applying hypothetical information to genuine world datasets, and acquiring pragmatic experience. Here are a few involved project thoughts for rehearsing AI:

1. Prescient Examination:

- ***Prescient upkeep:*** Construct an AI model to foresee hardware disappointments and timetable support proactively in view of sensor information from modern apparatus.

- ***Client beat expectation:*** Foster an AI model to foresee client stir in a membership based business utilizing verifiable client information and segment data.

2. Regular Language Handling (NLP):

- ***Opinion examination:*** Fabricate a feeling investigation model to group message information (e.g., item surveys, virtual entertainment posts) as good, pessimistic, or nonpartisan in view of feeling.

- ***Named element acknowledgment:*** Foster a named substance acknowledgment model to separate named substances (e.g., individual names, associations, areas) from unstructured text information.

3. PC Vision:

- ***Object discovery:*** Construct an article location model to recognize and confine objects of interest in pictures or recordings utilizing profound learning procedures, for example, convolutional brain organizations (CNNs).

- ***Facial acknowledgment:*** Foster a facial acknowledgment model to recognize and check people in pictures or recordings utilizing procedures like profound face acknowledgment.

AI has turned into an indispensable piece of different businesses, driving advancement, and empowering groundbreaking answers for complex issues. Genuine models and contextual analyses feature the assorted utilizations of AI across areas, including medical care, finance, online business, and transportation. Involved projects give significant chances to rehearsing AI abilities and acquiring reasonable experience by applying hypothetical information to genuine world datasets. By investigating genuine models, contextual investigations, and involved projects, people can acquire a more profound comprehension of AI applications and foster the abilities expected to prevail in this quickly developing field.

Conclusion

Recap and Key Takeaways

In this extensive aide, we take care of different parts of building an AI model, from understanding the fundamentals to sending the model in certifiable situations. We should recap the vital focal points and examine the subsequent stages in your AI process.

Recap:

1. *Figuring out the Fundamentals*: AI includes calculations that gain from information to pursue expectations or choices without being unequivocally customized. It envelops managed learning, unaided learning, and support learning strategies.

2. **Setting Up Your Current circumstance**: Setting up your advancement climate

with the right apparatuses and systems, like Python, TensorFlow, PyTorch, and scikit-learn, is fundamental for building and preparing AI models productively.

3. ***Information Arrangement***: Information readiness includes gathering, investigating, cleaning, and preprocessing information to guarantee its quality and appropriateness for preparing AI models. Key advances incorporate information assortment, investigation, cleaning, and preprocessing strategies like taking care of missing qualities, exception identification, and component scaling.

4. ***Model Preparation***: Model preparation includes choosing a proper calculation, dividing the information

for preparing and testing, and tuning hyperparameters for ideal execution. Key advances incorporate picking the right calculation, dividing information, tuning hyperparameters, and assessing model execution utilizing execution measurements and assessment strategies.

5. ***Arrangement and Then some:*** Sending the model in genuine situations includes framework arrangement, model bundling, combination with existing frameworks, testing and approval, observing, security, and consistence. Constant improvement includes observing the model's exhibition, gathering input, and iteratively further developing the model in light of client criticism and information quality.

Key Action items:

1. Begin with a strong comprehension of the essentials of AI, including various calculations, procedures, and systems.

2. Set up your advancement climate with the right instruments and structures, and work on coding and executing AI calculations on genuine world datasets.

3. Focus on information planning, as it is pivotal for guaranteeing the quality and reasonableness of the information for preparing AI models.

4. Explore different avenues regarding various calculations, hyperparameters, and assessment methods to track down the best model for your particular errand and space.

5. Send the model in certifiable situations, screen its exhibition, accumulate criticism, and ceaselessly further develop the model in light of client criticism and information quality.

Next Steps in Your Machine Learning Journey

1. **Extend Your Insight**: Keep learning and investigating progressed points in AI, for example, profound learning, support learning, regular language handling, and PC vision.

2. **Work on Active Activities**: Apply your insight and abilities to involved projects, like Kaggle contests, open-source commitments, or true issues in your area of interest.

3. **Remain Refreshed**: Remain informed about the most recent turns of events,

research papers, and headways in AI by following applicable websites, discussions, meetings, and examination distributions.

4. **Network and Team up**: Interface with other AI professionals, scientists, and aficionados through web-based networks, meetups, studios, and gatherings. Work together on projects, share thoughts, and gain from others in the field.

5. **Analyze and Improve**: Examination with groundbreaking thoughts, procedures, and strategies in AI, and investigate imaginative applications and use cases in your space of revenue.

Building an AI model requires a mix of hypothetical information, viable abilities, and involved insight. By grasping the fundamentals, setting up your current circumstance, dominating information planning, model preparation, organization, and persistent improvement, you can fabricate and convey viable AI models to take care of genuine issues and drive development in different businesses. As you proceed with your AI process, continue investigating, testing, and figuring out how to remain at the very front of this quickly developing field. Keep in mind, the potential outcomes with AI are perpetual, and your process is simply starting.